Ripley's SPACE
Believe It or Not!®

Ripley
PUBLISHING

a Jim Pattison Company

TWISTS

Written by Dr Mike Goldsmith
Consultant Clint Twist

PUBLISHING

Publisher Anne Marshall

Managing Editor Rebecca Miles
Picture Researcher James Proud
Editors Lisa Regan, Rosie Alexander
Assistant Editor Amy Harrison
Proofreader Judy Barratt
Indexer Hilary Bird

Art Director Sam South
Design Rocket Design (East Anglia) Ltd
Reprographics Stephan Davis

www.ripleys.com

ISBN 978-1-893951-48-8

10 9 8 7 6 5 4 3 2 1

Library of Congress Cataloging-in-Publication Data is available.

Printed in China

PUBLISHER'S NOTE
While every effort has been made to verify the accuracy of the entries in this book, the Publishers cannot be held responsible for any errors contained in the work. They would be glad to receive any information from readers.

WARNING
Some of the stunts and activities in this book are undertaken by experts and should not be attempted by anyone without adequate training and supervision.

Contents

PAGE 15

PAGE
22

PAGE
44

Universally Speaking

🌀 TOTALLY OUT THERE

Space is fascinating, and huge, and complicated. It's full of things you can see, like stars, and satellites, and the Sun. It's even more full of things you can't see, like black holes, and wormholes, and dark energy. Scientists have spent lifetimes trying to make sense of what's out there. How big is the Universe? How did it all begin? Where will it all end?

This book shows you some of space's best bits: shuttles and space stations, planets and probes, meteorites and moons, asteroids and astronauts. Every page is packed with out-of-this world info, with special Ripley's fascinating facts and amazing "Believe It or Not!" stories. Are you ready to read on? 5-4-3-2-1…

?

HERE TO HELP...
Of course, this book is packed full of fab facts and informative text —but look out for the five key features (numbered here). They will help you find out even more about space—fun, facts, stories, it's all here!

The galaxies appear to overlap but they may be at different distances from Earth.

Bright blue stars have been newly formed by the galaxies.

This type of galaxy is called a spiral galaxy because of its shape.

1

Sending telescopes into space allows astronomers to see things that aren't usually visible from Earth. This photo, taken by the Hubble Space Telescope (see page 35), is of three galaxies hundreds of light years from our planet.

TWISTS

It's not enough for some astronauts to go into space in a spaceship: they want to take a walk while they're there! A special protective suit (see page 40) allows EVA (extra-vehicular activity). The longest EVA was done in 2001 by two astronauts who stayed outside the International Space Station (see page 42) for nearly 9 hours.

(see page 40)
(see page 42)

twist it!

A Japanese company has developed space yogurt, for sale on Earth. The bacteria used to make the yogurt was blasted into space on a Soyuz rocket to enhance the flavor and any immunity-boosting powers.

If you traveled through the Universe in a spaceship, you would never reach the edge, no matter how fast or far or long you traveled in your spacecraft.

Feel like a trip into space? A firm in Florida will send you up there, when you die! Customers pay for the ashes of their loved ones to be launched to the lower layers of the atmosphere in a balloon and scattered at 30,000 feet.

I do

Cosmonaut Yuri Malenchenko and his fiancée Ekaterina Dmitriev got married by satellite link while he was serving as Commander of the International Space Station! They married in Texas, where weddings are allowed even if one party is absent—but the missing person isn't usually orbiting 240 miles above the Earth!

Smart stuff

SMART-1 is the first European spacecraft to orbit the Moon. It was launched in 2003 and used the same electric propulsion system as NASA's Deep Space 1 probe.

FASCINATING FACT! FASCINATING FACT! FASCINATING FACT!

5

Believe It or Not!

2

Who'd have thought it? Read all about some totally out there (but totally true) stories—like the teddies sent into space. Members of Cambridge University space-flight club launched four teds on a weather balloon. The teddies wore suits made of foil, foam, plastic bottles, and tape, which had been designed by schoolchildren to protect their furry friends from the -58°F temperatures.

Recipe time!

How to make a UNIVERSE

Mix up a Universe just like ours (you'll need a very large mixing bowl).
Ingredients:

- **Dark matter** Cold dark matter (approx. one quarter total amount)
- **Dark energy** Dark energy (roughly 70% total amount)
- **Gas** Plenty of gas (hydrogen works best, well seasoned with helium)
- **Dust** Dust (dust and gas both work well when gathered together into nebulae, but you'll need plenty more of each to sprinkle thinly through your whole Universe)
- **Stars** Ten billion trillion stars
- **Planets** Planets (you'll need around a dozen per star, so it's worth getting an economy pack for a whole Universe)
- **Objects** A few trillion trillion fun-size objects: dwarf planets, comets, meteoroids

Garnish of your choice for Earth-type planets: anything from people and animals to books, chips, and pants!

UPSIDE DOWN

3

Imagine you're floating in space and your book won't stay still. Don't worry: one of the TWISTS of this book is that some items are all over the place! Turn the book or let the effects of freefall do it for you...

SAY WHAT?

4

Space is full of complicated things, so if you're feeling lost, check out the definitions in these boxes. Words like cosmology: the study of the Universe and how it was formed.

HOW BiG?

THE UNIVERSE

These smudges of light are groups of millions of stars, billions of trillions of miles away. The time taken for their light to cross the Universe means this picture is a few billion years out of date!

If you traveled through the Universe in a spaceship, you would never reach an edge, no matter how fast or far or long you traveled!

Everything that exists is part of the Universe, and that's a big, big, big, place. HUGE! In fact, the distance across the Universe is at least an enormous 600 billion trillion miles. Many scientists think that it's larger than this: it may even go on for ever!

The Universe is expanding (getting bigger) every second.

The Universe contains more than a billion trillion stars, yet it is mostly empty space. All the stars and planets and other things we can see only make up about 5% of the Universe —the rest is called "dark energy" and "dark matter," and no one knows what they are!

The Universe has no center.

How big?

JUST HOW BIG IS 600 BILLION TRILLION MILES? EVEN ON THE PAGE IT'S AN ENORMOUS NUMBER:

600,000,000,000,000,000,000,000!

twist it!

The temperature of most of the Universe is −454°F, much colder than the coldest freezer on Earth, and only 5 degrees warmer than the coldest possible temperature.

Three-quarters of the known Universe (that is, other than dark matter and dark energy) is hydrogen.

Even on the clearest, darkest night you can see fewer than 1/100,000,000,000,000,000 (one-hundred thousand trillionth) of the stars in the Universe.

On average, the Universe contains only one atom in every five cubic yards. This is like one cube of sugar in a box with sides over 6,000 miles long.

It is possible that before our Universe existed there was another one, and another one before that, and another before that...

Ripley's Believe It or Not!

UP, UP AND AWAY

SpaceShipOne was the first private manned spacecraft in space (exceeding an altitude of 100,000 meters). In 2004 the craft was successfully launched twice within a two-week period, claiming the Ansari X prize of $10 million. The competition's aim was to boost civilian-led (rather than military-led) spaceflight. The team have joined forces with Virgin Galactic, intending to send customers into space on short trips.

seeing stars

Imagine waking up and seeing the stars above you! You don't need to sleep outdoors—artist Rip Read can paint a StarMural on your ceiling. The painting is only visible in the dark, so the "Startist" has to work at night, with the lights out!

SAY WHAT?

BILLION AND TRILLION

A billion is one thousand million, or 1,000,000,000. A trillion is even bigger: one million million, or 1,000,000,000,000. A billion trillion has 21 zeros on the end!

May the Force be with You

⊛ GRAVITY

floaters!

Gravity, the force that holds you to the ground, also stops the Earth falling apart, keeps the Moon going around the Earth, and the Earth going around the Sun.

The more massive the planet you stand on, the stronger gravity becomes, and the more you weigh. If you could stand on Jupiter you would weigh more than twice as much as on Earth, and on the Sun you would weigh a thundering 2 tons. On the Moon you would weigh so little that you would be a super-Olympian, jumping about four times higher than on Earth. In deep space, far from any star or planet, you would weigh zilch, zero, nothing at all.

When you are falling, you don't feel the pull of gravity, which is why astronauts in orbit are weightless, even though the Earth's gravity is nearly as strong in orbit as on the surface of the Earth. The astronauts are in a constant state of falling, but so is their spacecraft, so the astronauts float around inside.

⊛ **Everything** in the Universe pulls on everything else with the force of gravity—even you and this book are strangely attracted to each other!

⊛ **Near a black hole** (see page 30) the gravity is strong enough to tear you apart.

>> space surgery >>

In 2006, surgeons from Bordeaux University carried out an operation under weightless conditions, to practice for surgery in space.

FORCEFUL STUFF

If you could survive the heat in the center of the Earth, you would find that you weighed nothing there and could float around, because the gravity would pull you equally in all directions.

Time slows down where gravity is strong. So, if your parents spent a few decades near a black hole, they could be younger than you when they came home. This also means that people who live on mountains age faster than those living at sea level.

Neurolab was a 1998 space shuttle experiment to test the reactions of living creatures to weightless conditions. It contained 1,500 crickets, 230 swordtail fish, 130 water snails, 150 rats, and 18 pregnant mice.

The gravity on some asteroids (see page 24) is so low you could jump off them.

You weigh more at the Poles and less at the Equator, due partly to the Earth's shape and partly to its spin.

twist it!

Ripley's Believe It or Not!

Albert Einstein discovered that gravity is a warp (bend) in time and space. Einstein was one of the world's most famous scientists. He lived from 1879 to 1955 and developed the Theory of General Relativity, about how gravity works.

SAY HI to a robot Einstein! This US robot can act like a human in certain ways, such as having a conversation, recognizing faces, changing facial expressions, and mimicking emotions.

Hubo Lab
Humanoid Robot Research Center

KAIST

SAY WHAT?

ORBIT
The path of one object around another in space.

Paralympian Wojtek Czyz set a new long jump record in 2008, wearing a prosthetic leg made of space materials! The same material was used in his leg and in a spectrometer to be mounted on the ISS (International Space Station), as both items need to be extremely strong and light.

FASCINATING FACT

Vesta (asteroid) 204 feet

JUMP AROUND>>

Want to break the world high jump record? All you have to do is go to the Moon: our space-neighbor is much less massive than the Earth, which means the pull of gravity there is less, and so is your weight, so you could jump much higher than at home. To really impress the spectators, try jumping on an asteroid like Vesta. Don't forget to take some air with you.

Pluto 79 feet ►

Moon 30 feet ►

Mars 15 feet ►

Earth 8 feet ►

Home Truths

THE EARTH

As far as we know, Earth is the only place in the Universe where life exists. Though we live all over the place, some of our planet isn't too friendly: 71% is covered in water, and 97% of that water is too salty to drink. Temperatures at the Poles fall as low as –128°F, and in deserts they can rise to a blistering 136°F.

That's just on the surface—inside the Earth, it gets hotter as you go deeper. It reaches about 10,800°F in the core —about as hot as the surface of the Sun. In the other direction, up in the air, the temperature falls fast and you would freeze to death just a few miles up.

No one knows exactly how many individual living things there are on Earth, but it is at least 5 million trillion trillion—almost all of which are too small to see without a microscope.

OLD TIMER

Planet Earth is roughly a third of the age of the Universe (making Earth about 4.5 billion years old).

SAY WHAT?

POLES
The "ends" of a planet, around which it spins.

If you stood on the Earth's Equator, you would be spinning around with the Earth at 1,038 mph.

5 MILLION TRILLION TRILLION IS WRITTEN LIKE THIS 5,000,000,000,000,000,000,000,000,000,000,000 **THAT'S A WHOLE LOT OF ZEROS!**

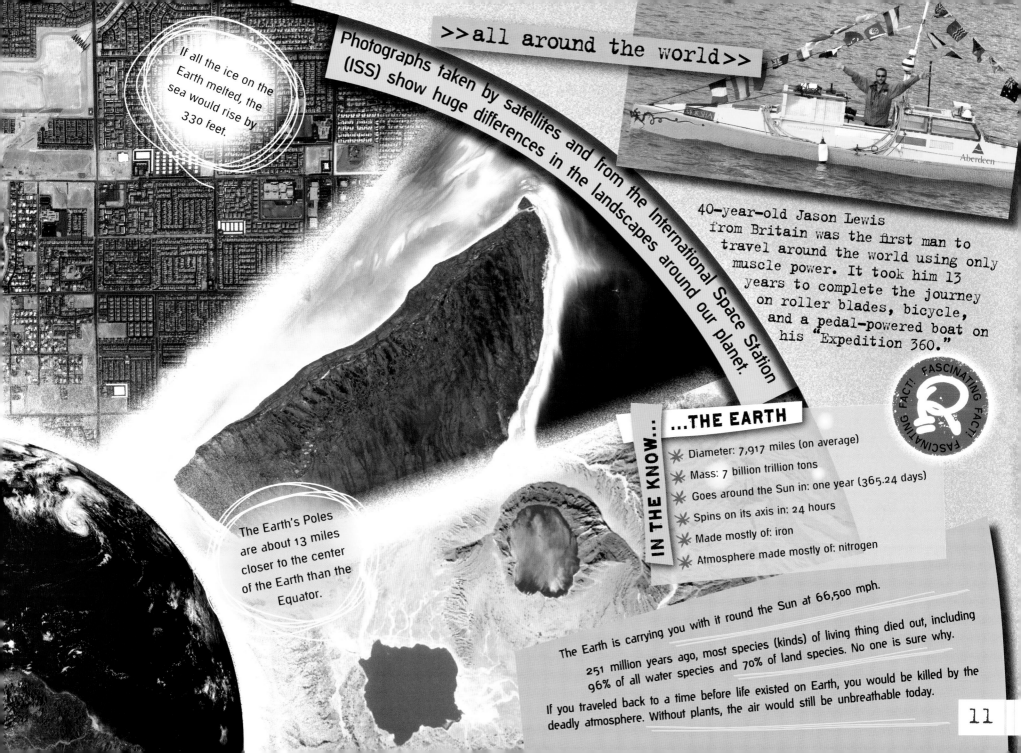

If all the ice on the Earth melted, the sea would rise by 330 feet.

Photographs taken by satellites and from the International Space Station (ISS) show huge differences in the landscapes around our planet.

40-year-old Jason Lewis from Britain was the first man to travel around the world using only muscle power. It took him 13 years to complete the journey on roller blades, bicycle, and a pedal-powered boat on his "Expedition 360."

The Earth's Poles are about 13 miles closer to the center of the Earth than the Equator.

IN THE KNOW...

...THE EARTH

* Diameter: 7,917 miles (on average)
* Mass: 7 billion trillion tons
* Goes around the Sun in: one year (365.24 days)
* Spins on its axis in: 24 hours
* Made mostly of: iron
* Atmosphere made mostly of: nitrogen

FASCINATING FACT! FASCINATING FACT!

The Earth is carrying you with it round the Sun at 66,500 mph.

251 million years ago, most species (kinds) of living thing died out, including 96% of all water species and 70% of land species. No one is sure why.

If you traveled back to a time before life existed on Earth, you would be killed by the deadly atmosphere. Without plants, the air would still be unbreathable today.

11

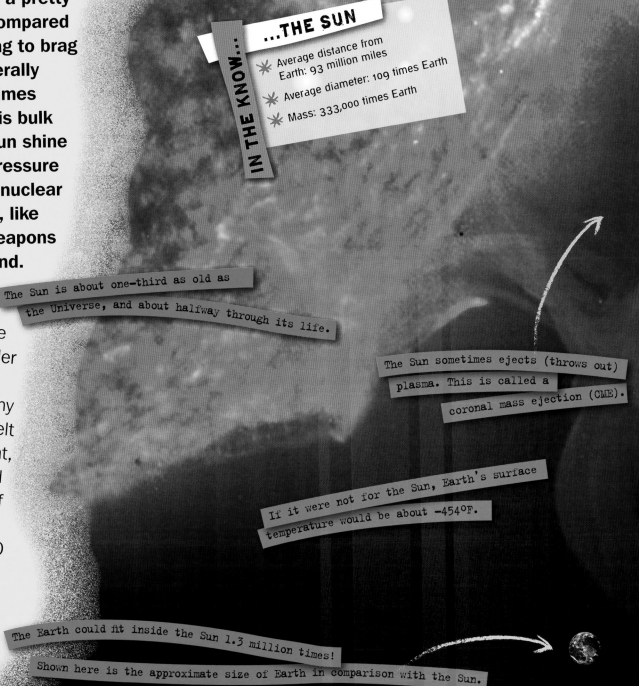

OurSensationalStar

The Earth seems like a pretty gigantic place, but compared to the Sun it's nothing to brag about. The Sun is literally massive—333,000 times the Earth's mass. This bulk is what makes the Sun shine —deep inside, the pressure is so enormous that nuclear reactions take place, like billions of nuclear weapons going off every second.

Even though the surface of the Sun is much cooler than the core, it's still 10,920°F: so hot that any metal on Earth would melt there. Yet, despite all that, the Sun is a very dull and ordinary star, like many of those in the sky. It is only the fact that it is 250,000 times closer to Earth than the next nearest star that makes it seem so bright.

IN THE KNOW... ...THE SUN

* Average distance from Earth: 93 million miles
* Average diameter: 109 times Earth
* Mass: 333,000 times Earth

The Sun is about one-third as old as the Universe, and about halfway through its life.

The Sun sometimes ejects (throws out) plasma. This is called a coronal mass ejection (CME).

If it were not for the Sun, Earth's surface temperature would be about −454°F.

The Earth could fit inside the Sun 1.3 million times!

Shown here is the approximate size of Earth in comparison with the Sun.

HERE COMES THE SUN

If the Sun suddenly vanished, we would see it in the sky for another eight minutes. This is the time it takes for sunlight to reach the Earth.

When the Sun begins to run out of fuel, it will grow so large and hot that it will melt the surface of the Earth.

The element helium was discovered on the Sun before it was found on Earth.

In 840, Emperor Louis of Bavaria died of fright caused by experiencing an eclipse of the Sun.

The Sun gives out enough energy in one second to supply the USA with energy for 50 million years! To produce this, it burns up an incredible 4 million tons of its mass. However, it will take about 5 billion years to burn it all up, so we needn't worry about it running out.

The Sun is 400 times bigger than our Moon but also 400 times farther away from the Earth.

The Sun outweighs the Earth by the same amount as 175 Boeing 747 planes to one person.

← twist it!

>>solar power>>

By harnessing the power of the Sun, a family in Montana, USA, spends only $20 a month on their fuel bills. Their aim was to build an environmentally friendly house without spending a fortune; 250 old tires and 13,000 empty soda cans were used in the building!

Ripley's Believe It or Not!

A pinhead-sized speck of the burning gases from our Sun could kill a man from 100 miles away.

Blackout

If the Moon moves between the Earth and the Sun, a solar eclipse occurs. Total eclipses are rare, and don't last long—usually less than seven minutes. In 1973 passengers on Concorde flew along with the Moon's moving umbra (shadow) and watched the eclipse for 74 minutes!

Lunar Tunes

OUR MOON

Average distance from Earth: 240,000 miles

Average diameter: 27% Earth

Mass: 1.2% of Earth

Length of day: 27 Earth days

It's around 240,000 miles away in space, but the Moon is the Earth's nearest neighbor—although it's as far away from home as humans have managed to get. It is an airless, lifeless ball of rocky mountains and plains of old lava but its effect on the Earth is massive—literally. Together with the Sun, it moves billions of tons of water each day, making the tides that wash every shore.

There are dozens of seas on the Moon, but no liquid water. The seas are areas of solidified lava (melted rock).

The beginning of the Moon was almost the end of the Earth: about 4.5 billion years ago, a planet-sized object smashed into our newly born world, and fragments from both planets made the Moon. If the object had been a little bigger, you wouldn't be here to read about it.

The Moon is getting farther away from you all the time: each full moon is 0.1 inch farther away than the last one.

14

FULL OF MOONS

The far side of the Moon was not seen until 1959, when a spacecraft sent a photo of it back to Earth. The Moon turns as it circles the Earth, always keeping the same face toward us.

In 1968, Russian tortoises flew around the Moon before returning safely to Earth in the Zond 5 spaceship.

The Moon contains mysterious areas called "mascons," which generate gravity strong enough to pull satellites off course.

If something happens "once in a blue moon" it could be more often than you think: a blue moon is the second of two full moons in one month, and occurs about once every 2¾ years. Don't get too excited—the Moon doesn't actually change color!

twist it!

Wish you were here!

Ripley's Believe It or Not!

Because there is no weather on the Moon, astronauts' footprints will survive for decades.

The US has successfully put people on the Moon six times. The first was in 1969 and the last was in 1972. Twelve astronauts have walked on the surface. Neil Armstrong was the first person to set foot on the Moon.

The massive costs involved in putting people on the Moon have prevented further government-funded missions. However, the Google Lunar X Prize offers $20 million to the first privately funded team to land a robotic probe on the Moon.

GETTING AWAY FROM IT ALL

Dutch architect Hans-Jurgen Rombaut has designed the first hotel intended for the Moon. It is supposed to be finished by 2050 and will have two tall, thin towers, extra-thick walls, and an insulating layer of water to keep out dangerous cosmic rays and regulate the temperature indoors.

GLITTER BALL

In 1992 the *Galileo* spacecraft, on its way to Jupiter, took pictures of the Moon using special color filters to record different substances making up the surface. When all the images are put together they give quite a different view—something more like a festive decoration than the Moon we see at night!

Hell Planets

MERCURY AND VENUS

Imagine a world where the Sun is six times brighter than usual, the sky is black, and the weather is hot enough to melt lead during the day and colder than a freezer at night. There is almost no air at all... This is what it is like on Mercury, the closest planet to our Sun.

MERCURY

On Mercury, a day lasts longer than a year.

The largest crater in the Solar System is on Mercury. Called Beethoven, it is 400 miles across.

Believe It or Not!

Seen from some parts of Mercury, the Sun rises twice a day at some times of the year. If you lived there, you would see the Sun rise about halfway up the sky, then reverse direction and set, before rising again and passing across the sky as usual.

IN THE KNOW...

...MERCURY

* Average distance from Sun: 36 million miles
* Diameter: 38% of Earth
* Mass: 5% of Earth
* Length of year: 88 Earth days
* Length of day: 176 Earth days

The first space probe to visit two planets, *Mariner 10* zoomed past Venus in 1974. It used the gravitational pull of Venus to change its orbit and head off to Mercury. Over 30 years later, *Messenger* has become only the second spacecraft to send back data about Mercury.

>> *Messenger* was launched on the night of August 3, 2004. >>

VENUS

IN THE KNOW...

Average distance from Sun: 67 million miles

✳ Diameter: 95% of Earth

✳ Mass: 82% of Earth

✳ Length of year: 225 Earth days

✳ Length of day: 117 Earth days

The highest volcano on Venus is called Maat Mons, and it rises 5 miles above the planet's surface. It is named after the Egyptian goddess of justice and truth. Every surface feature on Venus is named after a female, with just three exceptions.

SAY WHAT?

SULPHURIC ACID *Dangerous liquid which "eats away" many materials.*

Though farther from the Sun than Mercury, Venus is even hotter (about 860°F), because it is blanketed by a thick atmosphere. Without protection, you would die quickly, and not just from the heat: on Venus the air is deadly. Conditions on Venus are so extreme that no space probe that has managed to land there has survived for more than a few hours.

twist it!

The rain on Venus is made of sulphuric acid, but it boils away before it reaches the ground.

Venus has more dry land than anywhere else in the Solar System.

Venus spins backward, so the Sun rises in the West there—or it would if it were not too cloudy to see it.

On Venus, the sky is orange. On Mercury, it is black.

TOTALLY OUT THERE

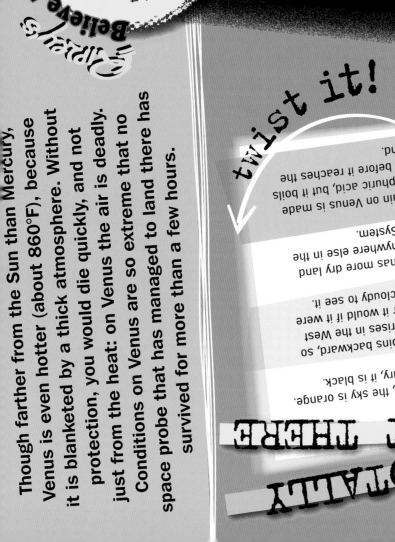

Red Planet

MARS

Mars is a harsh world of deserts and dust, red with rusted iron, but it would still win a "most similar planet to Earth" competition, with its icy poles, seasons, and 24.6-hour day. It used to be even more like home, with a thick atmosphere. Rivers once ran across the surface —and maybe living creatures did, too.

Since *Mariner 4* flew past in 1965, over 40 probes have been sent to explore Mars (more than to any other planet), and it is the next destination for human explorers. Despite the thin air on Mars, it does have weather—clouds, frost, dust-storms—but the last rainy day there was more than a million years ago.

Scientists use 3-D pictures like this one of the North Pole of Mars to work out the amount of water or ice there, and to study the surface and clouds.

On Mars, the sky is pink.

MARS

In the 19th century, creatures from Mars were usually called Martials.

Dust storms on Mars sometimes cover the whole planet.

Viking 1 landed here in 1976 and took photos of the surface of Mars.

WHEELIES!

In 1997 the first ever space robot rover *Sojourner* was equipped with automated programming so it could find its own way across the rocky surface of Mars. During its travels it sent over 17,000 photos back to scientists on Earth.

The Pathfinder robot had "laser eyes" starting to be roving on Mars, "roving" robot to be.

Sojourner

Pathfinder

Spirit on the surface of Mars.

IN THE KNOW... MARS

* Average distance from Sun: 142 million miles
* Diameter: 53.2% of Earth
* Mass: 11% of Earth
* Length of year: 687 Earth days
* Length of day: 24.6 hours

LIFE ON MARS

In 1938, the radio play *War of the Worlds* tricked people in the USA into believing Martians were invading Earth. Thousands of people fled the danger area.

Mars has the deepest canyon and the largest volcano in the Solar System. This volcano, Olympus Mons, is three times higher than Mount Everest and big enough to fit all of Hawaii's volcanic islands inside.

In 1911 a meteorite from Mars killed an Egyptian dog!

Phobos, one of Mars' moons, orbits only 5,827 miles from the planet—only 2.4% the distance at which the Moon orbits Earth.

Around 5,000 people (many of them NASA employees) belong to the Mars Society. They practice life on Mars by spending time in remote places, simulating the conditions they would expect on the red planet. Apparently, they wear helmets made from trash can lids and plastic light fixtures!

twist it!

Believe It or Not!

Scientists are keen to find out about water and ice on Mars as it may exist (or could exist) on the planet. NASA's 2003 rovers, *Spirit* and *Opportunity*, are still exploring the Martian surface and sending back information for whether life has existed on Mars. The cost of making and sending the rovers was said to be $820 million for the first 90-day planned mission!

Planet GIANTS

JUPITER AND SATURN

JUPITER

Jupiter and Saturn are the overweight giants of the Solar System—Jupiter is heavier than all the other planets put together. It has an enormously deep atmosphere full of multicolored storm clouds. It has 63 moons and is surrounded by a system of rings made of millions of pieces of rock.

- Jupiter gives out more heat than it gets from the Sun.

- In 1609, Italian scientist and astronomer Galileo Galilei used his new telescope to discover the four largest of Jupiter's moons.

- Many of Jupiter's moons orbit in the opposite direction to the planet's spin.

- Europa, a moon of Jupiter, is the smoothest world we know, with no hills or valleys.

Jupiter's Red Spot is a hurricane that has lasted for centuries. It is the biggest storm in the Solar System.

The Red Spot is 15,410 miles across—almost twice as wide as Earth. Wind speeds inside the storm reach 270 mph.

Believe It or Not!

Volcanoes on Io can throw out hot material at speeds of 0.6 miles per second. That's 20 times faster than the average volcano on Earth.

Io is the most volcanic place in the Solar System.

SATURN

The Earth could fit inside Saturn 1,321 times over. Like Jupiter, Saturn is shrouded by clouds, and no one knows exactly what lies beneath. It has many moons (about 61) including a weird cloudy moon called Titan, with air like car exhausts and, at least in places, a soft surface with a crispy coating. Saturn is famous for the rocky rings that surround it.

...SATURN

...IN THE KNOW...

* Average distance from Sun: 887 million miles
* Average diameter: 9 times Earth
* Mass: 95 times Earth
* Length of year: 29.5 Earth years
* Length of day: 10.7 hours

>>double shift>>

In 2008, the Cassini spacecraft completed its four-year mission to explore the Saturn system. It was still in good working order, so it was given a new "Equinox" mission, which will give scientists two more years to make more in-depth studies of Saturn and its rings.

Saturn is so light it would float in your bathtub (if you had a bathtub bigger than a planet, that is).

Some of Saturn's rings are kept in place by objects like small moons, called shepherds.

In 1610, Galileo discovered Saturn. His telescope wasn't good enough to see the rings properly and he thought they were moons. The next time he looked, they had disappeared! At a certain angle, the rings are "edge on" and so are hardly visible.

Saturn is about twice as far from the Sun as Jupiter is.

IceWorlds

◎ URANUS, NEPTUNE, AND PLUTO

Uranus is an ice giant. It is so far from the Sun that it is always colder there than the coldest Earth winter: about –328°F. A greenish-blue planet, it spins on its side following a collision (crash) with an unknown object billions of years ago.

Neptune is also huge and cold, about –346°F, and the fastest winds in the Solar System (over 1,200 mph). It is blue, with white clouds.

NEPTUNE

From Neptune, the Sun looks 1,096 times dimmer than it does from Earth.

Triton is Neptune's largest moon. It has active volcanoes, though it is the coldest world we know. The volcanoes are made of nitrogen.

There are places on Uranus where night lasts more than 40 Earth years.

...NEPTUNE

* Average distance from Sun: 2,794 million miles
* Average diameter: 3.9 times Earth
* Mass: 17 times Earth
* Length of year: 165 Earth years
* Length of day: 16.1 hours

URANUS

When William Herschel first discovered Uranus, he thought it was a comet.

...URANUS

* Average distance from Sun: 1,784 million miles
* Average diameter: 4 times Earth
* Mass: 15 times Earth
* Length of year: 84 Earth years
* Length of day: 17.2 hours

twist it!

You can't imagine Uranus spinning on its side (rather than spinning like a spinning top, like the other planets) then try to imagine it like a ball rolling along.

Neptune has still not been around the Sun once since it was discovered in 1846. It will finally complete its first orbit on June 8, 2011.

Neptune is so far from the Sun that it takes 165 Earth years to make one orbit, so if you were born there, you would not live long enough to celebrate your first birthday.

William Herschel wanted to call Uranus "George's Star," in honor of the British king, George III.

If you visited either of these planets and looked back toward the Sun, it would simply look like a bright star.

Neptune, the outermost planet in the Solar System, was tracked down through the effect of its gravity on the way Uranus moved, and not found until 1846.

The ice giants are so dim that Uranus was only discovered by accident in 1781.

FAR OUT

PLUTO

Pluto used to be called a planet, but is now officially a humble dwarf planet, one of three discovered so far. It usually orbits the Sun outside Neptune and is even colder, and mostly covered with frozen nitrogen gas.

- Pluto spins on its side, in a similar way to Uranus.

- Pluto was the ninth planet of our Solar System until the 2006 discovery of Eris, which forced astronomers to create a new definition of a true planet. The three dwarf planets are Pluto, Eris, and Ceres.

- Pluto's orbit isn't as circular as Neptune's, so although it is usually farther from the Sun, sometimes it changes position! Its orbit crosses inside that of Neptune for about 20 years in every 248.

- The coldest place on Earth (in Antarctica) has an average temperature about four times higher than Pluto's daytime temperature. Brrr!

>>new horizons >>

A spacecraft called New Horizons is on its way to Pluto. It was the fastest spacecraft ever launched, traveling at about 10 miles per second soon after it blasted off in 2006. It passed Jupiter in 2007 and is due to reach Pluto in 2015. It will be the first ever spacecraft to study Pluto.

23

DangerZone

SAY WHAT?

ASTEROID
A small rocky body in orbit around the Sun. Many asteroids are located between the orbits of Mars and Jupiter. These are the building blocks of a planet that failed to form there.

ASTEROIDS AND COMETS

Comets are like giant, dirty snowballs. Usually comets are fairly happy orbiting far out at the edge of the Solar System, about four trillion miles from Earth, but sometimes they swoop in toward the Sun, growing tails of gas and dust as they warm up.

If you've ever seen a comet, you probably weren't afraid—after all, it was just a whitish streak in the sky. Don't be fooled, though: comets can kill. In fact, it was probably a comet (or perhaps an asteroid) that wiped out the mighty dinosaurs 65 million years ago. It crashed into the Earth and the dust it threw up froze the planet, which killed the dinosaurs. And it could happen again—to us.

In 2000, Comet Hyakutake had a tail 342 million miles long nearly four times longer than the distance from the Earth to the Sun!

The center of a comet is called its nucleus.

Whooosh...

Comets are made of ice, dust, and rocky material that came from the Solar System when it was first created about 4.5 billion years ago.

twist it!

In 1908, a strange explosion flattened 830 sq miles of forest in Siberia. It was probably caused by a comet exploding in the air.

If you had been around in 1910, when the Earth passed through the tail of a comet, you could have tried some of the anti-comet pills that were on sale. They wouldn't have done you any good, though!

Halley is a comet that reappears every 75.3 years. There are records of its visits that go back to May 25, 240BC.

A comet called Shoemaker-Levy 9 crashed into Jupiter in 1994. It hit the planet on the side that was facing away from Earth, so the impact itself wasn't seen, but huge marks could be seen in Jupiter's atmosphere for several months afterward.

A comet or asteroid the size of a city crashed into Mexico's Yucatan Peninsula 65 million years ago.

Ripley's Believe It or Not!

Most comets have two streaming tails: a blue one made of gas and a white one made of dust.

This colossal crater, seen here from space, in Australia's Northern Territory is called Gosses Bluff and is about 2.8 miles wide. It was made by an asteroid or comet about 0.6 miles across that crashed into Earth around 142 million years ago.

FASCINATING FACT! FASCINATING FACT! FASCINATING FACT!

amazing!!

Trash!

SPACE RUBBLE AND JUNK

There are thousands of pieces of space junk in orbit around Earth. Space junk includes items such as broken satellites, parts of rockets, and even garbage thrown from space staions. There are also around 6,000 artificial satellites.

Building a solar system isn't a tidy job: after gravity pulled together our Sun and the planets, trillions of grains of dust and lumps of rock were left hanging about in space. There is a ring of scattered rubble between Mars and Jupiter called the asteroid belt, and even more rubble beyond Neptune.

Most of this rubble keeps itself to itself, but some of it falls through our atmosphere. If it is small enough, it drifts down to Earth and just makes everything a bit dustier. Bigger chunks burn up as meteors (shooting stars), and a few reach the ground as meteorites.

The first TV satellite was launched in 1964 to allow the Tokyo Olympics to be transmitted around the world.

Ripley's Believe It or Not!

Think you've seen a flying saucer? It could just be the reflection of the Sun off a satellite!

This artist's impression shows all the satellites (drawn larger than actual size) orbiting Earth.

TRASH CRASH

The first major collision between two satellites happened in February, 2009, when an old Russian satellite crashed into a working US satellite and created at least 600 more pieces of space junk.

LETHAL CLOTHING

In 1965 the US astronaut Edward White lost a glove while on a space walk from Gemini 4. It remained in orbit for a month, reaching speeds of 17,400 mph, and posed a lethal danger to spacecraft.

PUTTING OUT THE TRASH

The Mir space station threw more than 200 garbage bags into space over ten years. They are all still in orbit.

POW!

Space junk travels extremely fast, which makes it highly dangerous. At a speed of 17,000 mph a tiny speck hitting an astronaut on a space walk would have the same impact as a bullet.

METEORIC!

The Skylab space station created a spectacular meteor shower over Australia when it crashed to Earth in 1979.

The oldest man-made debris hurtling around our planet is the US satellite Vanguard. It was launched in 1958 and is still up there today.

For centuries, people living in Greenland made their tools out of three large meteorites, which were almost pure iron.

Asteroids were once thought to be fragments of an exploded planet.

About 500 meteorites crash to Earth each year, but only about five of these are found and reported to scientists. So you'll be fairly famous if you find one and hand it in.

Some meteorites began life on the Moon or Mars and were thrown into space by volcanoes before drifting through space to land on Earth.

twist it!

Mrs Hewlett Hodges from Alabama, USA, has actually been hit by a meteorite! It crashed through her roof, bounced off a radio, and hit her on the hip. Ouch!

ACTUAL SIZE!

Scientists have only three rock samples from other objects in our Solar System. They are from the Moon, Mars, and this piece of the asteroid Vesta, which fell to Earth as a meteorite.

>>shooting from the hip>>

Looking Up

THIS STAR CLUSTER IS HIDDEN FROM SIGHT BY INTERSTELLAR DUST, BUT CAN BE SEEN WITH INFRARED TELESCOPES.

STARS

How many stars do you think you can see in the night sky? A million? A billion? Actually, even on the darkest, clearest night, fewer than 3,000 are visible. This is only a tiny fraction of the mind-numbing total number, which is at least 70 billion trillion—said to be more than all the grains of sand on all the beaches in the world.

Some stars you can see are as big and bright as our Sun—and some are much bigger. Many stars are double, each spinning around the other. Many stars have planets, too. Stars usually last for billions of years—but the more massive they are, the brighter they burn and the shorter they live.

These stars make up one of the most massive star clusters in the Milky Way galaxy.

This is the remains of a supernova explosion (see page 30).

The red stars are supergiants, and the blue ones are young or newly formed stars.

ORION

CANIS MAJOR

GEMINI

TAURUS

Scientists think that new stars are formed inside nebulae (the plural of a nebula) such as this one. A nebula is a cloud full of dust and gas; when it gets squashed, parts of it get so hot that they become newborn stars.

star stories

Constellations are groups of stars that, from the Earth, look close to each other. They may really be huge distances apart in space, but they line up to form patterns that have been given names through history.

Orion, or The Hunter, is instantly recognizable by the three central stars making his "belt."

Canis Major, one of Orion's "hunting dogs," contains Sirius, the brightest star in our sky. It is about 25 times brighter than the Sun.

The constellation of **Gemini** is one of the signs of the zodiac. It looks like a pair of twins and can be seen around the world between December and March.

Taurus is also known as The Bull. It contains the Pleiades (say "play-uh-dees") star cluster and is visible between November and February.

Ripley's Believe It or Not!

Seeing double

About half of the stars in the Universe exist in pairs. They are called binary stars, and both orbit around the same point.

twist it!

The light from most stars you can see takes decades to get to the Earth, which means you are seeing them as they were before you were born.

Some brown dwarf stars are cooler than burning houses.

The star with the longest name is Shurnarkabtishashutu, which is Arabic for "under the southern horn of the bull."

If the Earth were the size of a marble, the nearest star would be 18,640 miles away.

The largest known star, VY Canis Majoris, is big enough to contain about 100 billion objects the size of the Sun.

STAR TURNS

Celebrities as diverse as Will Young, Britney Spears, Harrison Ford, Bruce Lee, Brooklyn Beckham, and even the Clintons and the Bushes have had stars named for them! Scientists give stars a name made up of letters and numbers (such as HD172167) but fans and celebrities themselves can pay to have their name given to a specific star.

StarDeath

When the Sun runs out of fuel, it will swell up and melt the Earth's surface —but there's no rush to leave home; it won't happen until about the year 5,000,000,000. Stars more than five times as massive as the Sun explode as supernovas, shining more brightly than a whole galaxy of stars.

Supernovas leave behind shrunken remains, and sometimes those remains are black holes. Why are they black? Because they even suck in light—nothing in the Universe can escape them. Not that you would need to worry about escaping —you'd be torn apart by the strong gravity well before you reached the hole itself.

This jet is lots of high-energy particles being blasted away by the black hole.

* The black hole at the center of this galaxy (called Centaurus A) has a mass one billion times more than our Sun.

* Centaurus A is really two galaxies in collision. It is full of new stars that are forming as a result. Trillions of tons of material from both galaxies is gradually being sucked into the black hole.

* Scientists can study this black hole and galaxy more easily than many others as it is relatively close to the Earth. It is about 14 million light-years from us, which means that the light from Centaurus A takes about 14 million years to reach us. One light-year is about 6 trillion miles.

5 BILLION YEARS AGO
Nebula shrinks under its own gravity and stars begin to form

PROTOSTAR: temperat rises, nuclear reactions start insi to stabilize star

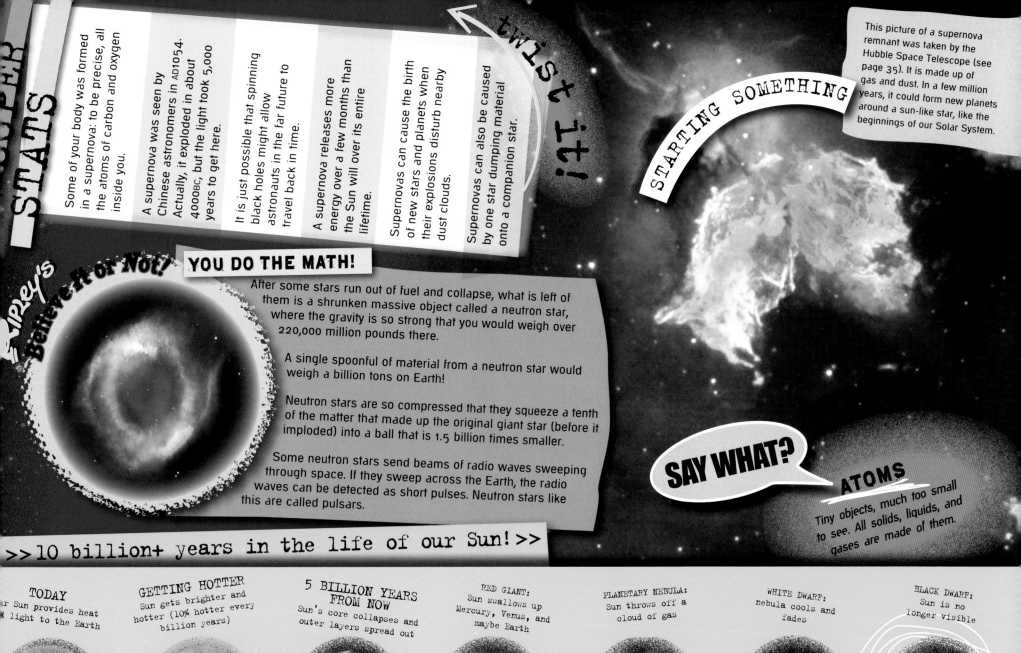

SUPER STATS

Some of your body was formed in a supernova: to be precise, all the atoms of carbon and oxygen inside you.

A supernova was seen by Chinese astronomers in AD1054. Actually, it exploded in about 4000BC, but the light took 5,000 years to get here.

It is just possible that spinning black holes might allow astronauts in the far future to travel back in time.

A supernova releases more energy over a few months than the Sun will over its entire lifetime.

Supernovas can cause the birth of new stars and planets when their explosions disturb nearby dust clouds.

Supernovas can also be caused by one star dumping material onto a companion star.

twist it!

STARTING SOMETHING

This picture of a supernova remnant was taken by the Hubble Space Telescope (see page 35). It is made up of gas and dust. In a few million years, it could form new planets around a sun-like star, like the beginnings of our Solar System.

Ripley's Believe It or Not!

YOU DO THE MATH!

After some stars run out of fuel and collapse, what is left of them is a shrunken massive object called a neutron star, where the gravity is so strong that you would weigh over 220,000 million pounds there.

A single spoonful of material from a neutron star would weigh a billion tons on Earth!

Neutron stars are so compressed that they squeeze a tenth of the matter that made up the original giant star (before it imploded) into a ball that is 1.5 billion times smaller.

Some neutron stars send beams of radio waves sweeping through space. If they sweep across the Earth, the radio waves can be detected as short pulses. Neutron stars like this are called pulsars.

SAY WHAT?

ATOMS
Tiny objects, much too small to see. All solids, liquids, and gases are made of them.

>>10 billion+ years in the life of our Sun! >>

TODAY
Our Sun provides heat and light to the Earth

GETTING HOTTER
Sun gets brighter and hotter (10% hotter every billion years)

5 BILLION YEARS FROM NOW
Sun's core collapses and outer layers spread out

RED GIANT:
Sun swallows up Mercury, Venus, and maybe Earth

PLANETARY NEBULA:
Sun throws off a cloud of gas

WHITE DWARF:
nebula cools and fades

BLACK DWARF:
Sun is no longer visible

Getting Together

Stars are gathered together throughout the Universe in groups called galaxies. Our own one is the Milky Way and it is made of about 300 billion stars (give or take a hundred billion)—so all the stars you can see on the darkest night add up to less than 0.000001% (or one-ten-millionth) of the whole thing.

Last century, astronomers noticed something very odd—most other galaxies are hurtling away from ours, and from each other, too. They realized that the whole Universe is getting bigger every second, and that everything in the Universe must have been crunched up together long ago. Very, very long ago (13.7 billion years to be precise), when it all began as a sudden expansion —the Big Bang.

NO PLACE LIKE HOME

Our Solar System is here.

- Our Solar System is perched between two arms of the Milky Way.

- If you counted one star a second and never slept, it would still take you about 3,000 years to count the stars in our galaxy.

- Long ago, most galaxies were blue, because of all the young stars being born in them.

- There are different types of galaxies, named according to their shape. The Milky Way is a spiral galaxy—it's not hard to see why.

Ripley's — Believe It or Not!

The Milky Way looks brighter from the Southern Hemisphere, because the southern part of our planet points roughly toward the star-packed center of our Galaxy. We live out in the suburbs, near the galactic edge, and can look out on the stars around us. If we lived near the center, the sky would be packed with stars, and the starlight would be brighter than the light of the full Moon. But, as there is a massive black hole in those parts, you might not have long to enjoy the view.

Most scientists think the expansion will go on for ever, even after the stars have all died and the Universe is cold. They call this the Big Chill. But some scientists think that, in about the year 50,000,000,000, everything will fall apart. First galaxies will be torn apart, then stars, then planets, then you (if you're still around, which is a bit unlikely) and finally atoms: the Big Rip.

twist it!

It takes about 225 million years for our Sun to revolve (move in a circle) once around the center of the galaxy.

You, along with the rest of our galaxy, are being dragged through space at about 1.25 million miles an hour by a mysterious unknown object called the Great Attractor. It's hidden from us by dust clouds.

Our galaxy is on a collision course with the Andromeda galaxy, but the galaxies won't meet until after our Sun has died.

The nearest large galaxy to the Milky Way is the Andromeda galaxy: it is so far away that its light takes 2.5 million years to reach us, and it is the furthest thing you can see with your naked eye.

GALACTIC TRIVIA

BIG BANG FACTS

Astronomers see back to almost the beginning of time when they look at quasars. Quasars are very bright objects (caused by various things falling into supermassive black holes) that can be seen across vast distances. To cross those distances, their light takes nearly as long as the age of the Universe.

For hundreds of thousands of years after it formed, the Universe was dark.

The Big Bang wasn't an explosion—space was only created when it happened, so there was nowhere for it to explode into!

Most of the atoms in your body are hydrogen, which formed very soon after the Big Bang—so most of you is almost as old as the Universe.

The Universe is more than a hundred million times older than the oldest person.

The most distant objects in the Universe are moving away from us at over 174,000 miles per second.

Star Gazing

TELESCOPES

Telescopes allow astronomers to see objects so far away that their light takes billions of years to reach us. Many telescopes gather light using huge mirrors, which is then focused by a lens. Some of these mirrors are ten million times the size of your pupils, which are what you use to gather light. They can collect light for hours on end (which your eyes can't).

There are also telescopes that detect "light" that we can't see at all—like radio waves, infra-red, ultraviolet, X-rays, and gamma rays. So, if you want to have a good look around outer space, take some advice— use a telescope.

These images were all obtained by the Spitzer Space Telescope.

These are the "Pillars of Creation," huge pillars of space dust lit by new stars.

This orange disc is the dying remains of a huge star, which exploded thousands of years ago.

The "Trifid Nebula" is a giant cloud of gas and dust where stars form.

The top of Mauna Kea (a volcano in Hawaii) is home to 13 telescopes owned and run by astronomers from 11 countries (including Japan, Canada, France, the UK, and the USA). The site has more cloud-free nights than most other suitable places around the world.

This is Mauna Lao, the world's largest volcano.

STARING INTO SPACE

The Spitzer Space Telescope was launched in 2003 and orbits the Earth, taking infrared pictures to help scientists study how galaxies are formed and develop. Infrared is heat radiation, so the telescope has to be kept cool so that its own heat doesn't interfere with the signals it receives from space.

LOOK OUT!

The most powerful telescopes can see so far away, the light started traveling billions of years ago. They show us galaxies as they looked less than one billion years after the beginning of the Universe.

The largest radio telescope dish in the world is at Arecibo, Puerto Rico. It is 1,000 feet across.

Italian scientist Galileo Galilei built one of the first telescopes in 1609. Within a few nights he had discovered mountains on the Moon, four moons of Jupiter, and hundreds of unknown stars.

The nearest star is about one million times farther from Earth than the nearest planet.

The highest speed in the Universe is the speed of light, which is 186,282 miles per second. It would take over four years to reach the nearest star even at this speed. But don't bother trying to go that fast; the faster you go, the more massive you get, and you would weigh more than the Universe by the time you got close to light speed.

twist it!

Ripley's Believe It or Not!

The Hubble Space Telescope (HST) orbits the Earth so that its view of the Universe is not interrupted by the atmosphere (like ground-based telescopes). It can see a coin 435 miles away!

SAY WHAT?

PUPIL The dark hole in the middle of each eye, through which light enters.

The Very Large Array (VLA) is an arrangement of 27 large radio telescopes in New Mexico, USA. Each one measures 82 feet across (about the size of a house). They are all mounted on tracks so they can be moved into different positions, but work together to act like one large radio telescope.

VERY LARGE INDEED

Observatories with telescopes inside.

Into the Unknown

Saturn V Rocket

As tall as St Paul's Cathedral in London; higher than the Statue of Liberty!

364 feet tall (including *Apollo* spacecraft).

Looking at the stars, it's hard to imagine what it's like in space. Telescopes allow us to see what's up there in much more detail. But there's nothing like getting up close and personal, and that's what the invention of spaceships has done for humans—and for the various animals that have been blasted into space for research purposes.

The first space orbit was by the Russian artificial satellite, *Sputnik*, in 1957. The first human in space was also Russian, Yuri Gagarin, who orbited the Earth in 1961. The rivalry between the USA and Russia (then called the Soviet Union) drove both countries on in the "Space Race" to achieve milestones in all areas of space exploration. Many people think that putting man on the Moon, in 1969, made the US the ultimate winners. Nowadays, international cooperation allows us to find out more about our Universe than ever before.

...SATURN V

* First manned flight: December, 1968
* Last flight: December, 1972
* Total launches: 13
* Total made: 15 (2 were unused)

IN THE KNOW...

Base has five engines, positioned like the five dots on dice.

33 feet wide.

On their Moon missions were the biggest and most powerful launch vehicles ever used.

Each Saturn V rocket carried enough fuel to fill an Olympic swimming pool, and used it up in 2.5 minutes.

There were three stages in a Saturn V rocket. Each stage separated and fell away after use. The third stage fired twice: to enter orbit and to change its path to head toward the Moon.

The 2008 movie *Space Chimps*

was based on a true story! Well, perhaps —the main character, Ham III, is the supposed grandson of a real chimp called Ham, who was launched into space in 1961. Ham was sent up in a *Project Mercury* capsule as part of the research needed for human space travel. He landed successfully in the ocean after the flight, and lived until 1983 at North Carolina Zoo.

>> FIRSTS >>

In 1961, Yuri Gagarin (USSR) became the first human being ever in space, and the first to orbit the Earth. The first people to see him upon his return were two Russian farm workers, Anna and Rita Takhtarov, who must have been quite surprised to see him emerge into a field from his landing craft.

Ripley's Believe It or Not!

The Russian *Soyuz* series of spacecraft first flew in 1966 and is still operating today, carrying astronauts to the International Space Station. *Soyuz* rockets have launched more human spaceflight missions than any other space program.

To Boldly Go

EXPLORATION

All modern spaceships are launched from Earth using liquid-fueled rockets. The first of these took off in 1926 and reached a height of just over 39 feet. Impressive? No, but 43 years later, a liquid fuel rocket carried three men 30,000 times farther—to the Moon. The 1960s and 1970s was an era of giant rockets, with giant price tags, and they could be used only once. From the 1980s a less costly vehicle has been used and re-used: the space shuttle.

A space shuttle does exactly what it says—shuttles satellites to space and people to the International Space Station (ISS). Russian Soyuz spacecraft go there, too, and one Soyuz craft is always docked at the ISS just in case an emergency getaway is needed.

External fuel tank

Solid Rocket Booster (SRB)

Cockpit

Orbiter

Rudder

Engine nozzle

Elevons for control

Atlantis

United States

The space shuttle blasts off.

The shuttle lands back on Earth.

The spent fuel tank falls away.

After launch, the shuttle starts to twist into an arc ready to enter orbit.

126 seconds after launch, the thin white rocket boosters are pushed away from the shuttle.

Next, the brown fuel tank falls away and burns up as it re-enters the Earth's atmosphere.

When the mission ends, the shuttle orbiter glides back to Earth and lands like an airplane.

twist it!

The first rocket flight in 1926 was of a liquid-fueled rocket invented by Robert Goddard of Massachusetts, USA. He launched it on his Aunt Effie's farm and after reaching 39¼ feet, it landed in a cabbage field.

5-4-3-2-1

England's "Astronomer Royal" said in 1956 that "Space travel is utter bilge." The first satellite was launched the following year. How embarrassing!

The first space traveler was a dog called Laika, who was sent into space in 1957.

Once they're well away from Earth and other large objects, spaceships can keep moving without using any fuel at all.

The fastest humans were the astronauts on the Apollo 10 mission, who reached 24,791 mph on their way back to Earth in 1969.

The engine that powers a space shuttle is as powerful as 39 train engines, yet is only one-seventh of the weight. In 25 seconds it can pump enough fuel to fill a swimming pool, and the overall power of a space shuttle at takeoff is equivalent to 16 million horsepower. Despite this, the humble flea can accelerate about 50 times faster.

In 2009, a bat blasted off on the side of space shuttle *Discovery*'s external tank. No one knows how long it managed to hold on for.

A 1995 space-shuttle launch was delayed by woodpeckers, who pecked holes in its fuel tank.

HITCHING A RIDE

Ripley's Believe It or Not!

After landing, the space shuttle orbiter is fastened onto the back of a Boeing 747 plane to be flown back to the launch site, ready for its next mission.

> > BLAST OFF! < <

Sky Workers

ASTRONAUTS

Space is a dangerous place: there's no air there, and it's full of deadly radiation. In the sunlight, it's hotter than an oven; in the shadows it's colder than a freezer. An unprotected person would be dead in seconds.

So, to venture into space, people have to be sealed into spacesuits, and the suits have to be warmed, cooled, pressurized, and supplied with fresh air. It's no wonder a spacesuit takes over six hours to put on, and costs well over a million dollars.

"Backpack" contains breathable oxygen.

Each mission has its own insignia (logo) on a badge.

Jet pack allows astronaut to fly back to International Space Station (ISS) in an emergency.

Inner suit (like underwear) is temperature controlled.

SUITS YOU!

Legs and arms have special suit joints to allow more movement.

Boots have metal rings at the top to alter their size for different astronauts.

Living in weightless conditions for weeks and months takes its toll on the human body. Astronauts have to exercise every day to keep their muscles strong.

It can be tricky using a toolbox in space—your screwdriv floats away! To help with ordinary maintenance, astronauts use velcro belts to keep their tools on hand, and hook their feet under straps or bars to stop themselves from drifting around.

Astronauts only wear special spacesuits for takeoff and landing, or when they leave the ISS. The rest of the time, they wear normal clothes like shorts and T-shirts.

Astronauts wear this orange suit for launch and landing. It's called an LES: Launch and Entry Suit.

Space Diary

Get up at 6am GMT. We're allowed 90 minutes "post-sleep" to wash, dress, eat breakfast, maybe exercise, and be ready to start work.

DPC (daily planning conference) with ground control center for 15 mins, to confirm the day's actions. My job today is unpacking supplies brought by the shuttle.

I think tomorrow will be science experiments, and at the weekend I get time to myself. Will hook up with my family on a video link (until the signal dies!). Most mornings I manage to use the treadmill or the exercise bike, too.

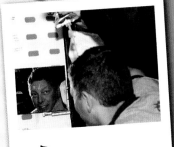

Lunch break is an hour, and the crew all eat together. Warm up my food and take the chance to take photos out of the Service Module windows. Earth looks amazing from up here!

More ground support links in the afternoon to check that all is going to plan. Have to do our chores even up in space! We have a new toilet system for one of the guys to activate, and I need to finish that unpacking. Everything has its proper place!

Finish work at 6pm and unwind over dinner with the others. Time to catch up on some reading, emails, or just gazing at the views. We have movies for the weekends, and tuck ourselves into bed about .30 (although sometimes we stay p later!).

When it's bedtime, astronauts climb nto sleeping bags, which are fixed to the wall, and hook their arms into restraints to stop them from floating around in their sleep.

Astronauts often wash with a damp cloth to reduce the amount of water used on the ISS.

Food is often warmed in a microwave and eaten from a special tray that stops everything from floating away.

It isn't easy using the toilet in space! The waste gets sucked away and put in bags for disposal. On spacewalks, astronauts wear adult diapers as they can be outside the ISS for hours.

twist it!

SPACED OUT

There is no up (and no down) in space.

If you were an astronaut in orbit, you would see the Sun rise and set 15 times a day, because of your speedy motion around the Earth.

Astronauts can't shed tears in space, so it's an ideal place to peel onions!

In 2001, orbiting astronauts took delivery of a pizza! It wasn't delivered by a person on a moped though...

The longest spacewalk took 8 hours and 29 minutes. It was made by shuttle astronauts who were dealing with a faulty satellite.

Astronauts grow 2 inches when they are in space, because their backbones are no longer squashed by the Earth's gravity.

Half of all space-travelers get space-sick.

Ripley's —— Believe It or Not!

FOR SALE

During a spacewalk to retrieve two broken satellites, American astronaut Dale Gardner had his photo taken offering to sell them to anyone interested! The picture was taken by his fellow astronaut Joseph Allen, who can be seen in the reflection on Gardner's visor.

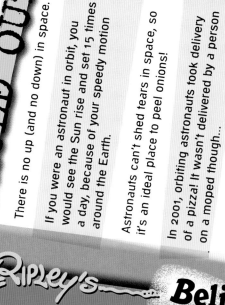

SPACE AGE

John Glenn was the first American to orbit the Earth, in 1962. He went back into space in 1998 onboard the shuttle Discovery, making him the oldest person (aged 77) to fly in space.

Action Stations

 ## LIFE IN SPACE

It's a long, long, way to the stars: if you were at the wheel of the fastest racing car there is, and if it could drive to the stars, how long do you think it would take to get there? A year? A century? How about 4 million years! That's just to the nearest star—most of the ones you can see are much farther away.

However, that doesn't mean people will never reach them. The plans for the first starship have already been made: a spaceship the size of a city, that will fly for a hundred years. In the meantime, astronauts can live in space for months at a time, on the International Space Station (ISS) that is being constructed in space over years and years.

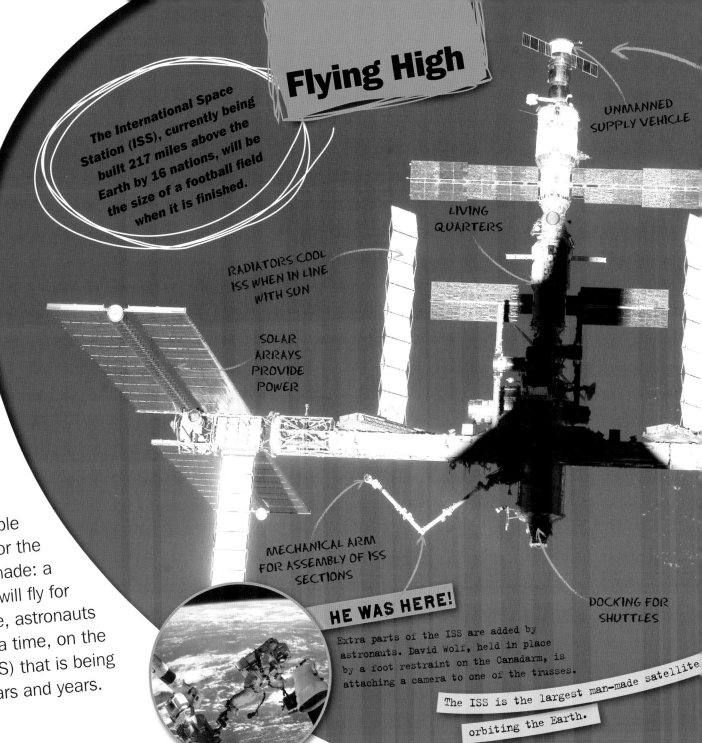

Flying High

The International Space Station (ISS), currently being built 217 miles above the Earth by 16 nations, will be the size of a football field when it is finished.

UNMANNED SUPPLY VEHICLE

LIVING QUARTERS

RADIATORS COOL ISS WHEN IN LINE WITH SUN

SOLAR ARRAYS PROVIDE POWER

MECHANICAL ARM FOR ASSEMBLY OF ISS SECTIONS

DOCKING FOR SHUTTLES

HE WAS HERE!

Extra parts of the ISS are added by astronauts. David Wolf, held in place by a foot restraint on the Canadarm, is attaching a camera to one of the trusses.

The ISS is the largest man-made satellite orbiting the Earth.

Three to four times a year, the unmanned Progress robot vehicle docks with the ISS to deliver food, water, and fuel, and take away the trash. It burns up as it re-enters Earth's atmosphere. True waste disposal!

What's this? Believe it or not, it's a photo of London at night, taken from the ISS. The wiggly line around the bottom edge is the highway, and the dark patches just below and left of the central bright section are Hyde Park and Regent's Park.

In 2006, a golf ball hit by cosmonaut Mikhail Tyurin entered Earth's orbit. It may still be traveling around the Earth even now! If not, it will fall toward Earth and burn up when it enters the atmosphere. It was hit off the ISS from a special tee attached to a platform, and will probably cover a distance of a billion miles. Now THAT'S a long shot!

NO SPACE LIKE HOME

Prior to the ISS, both the USA and Russia had working space stations orbiting the Earth. Skylab (USA) in the 1970s had three crew visits, while Russia's Salyut (1971–82) led to the more successful Mir space station.

In 1869 the first story was published about a space station—made of bricks! It was The Brick Moon by Edward Everett Hale.

The longest spaceflight was by the Russian cosmonaut Valeriy Polyakov, who stayed on space station Mir for 437 days.

Sections of the ISS are taken into space on board the shuttles Endeavor, Atlantis, and Discovery and the Russian crafts Proton and Soyuz. The first stages were joined together in orbit in 1998.

twist it!

Ripley's Believe It or Not!

In a Spin

Two spiders called Arabella and Anita were kept on the Skylab space station to study the effect of weightlessness on their ability to spin webs. It obviously took its toll, as the spiders spun uneven webs that weren't as strong as the ones they spun before takeoff.

IN THE KNOW...

...ISS

* Width: approx. 300 feet
* Length: approx. 245 feet
* Mass when finished: 992,000 pounds
* First launch: November 20, 1998
* Number of orbits per day: 15.7
* Traveling speed: 90,880 mph

LONG SHOT

Aliens are Coming!

FOR REAL?

Stephen Michalak said he found a UFO at Falcon Lake, Manitoba, Canada, in 1967. As he got closer he appeared to have been burned with a pattern of dots on his chest.

Signs of life

Two Italian professors have found signs of life from outer space! These micro-organisms were discovered concealed inside meteorites, and when put under lab conditions, they began to move and reproduce. Can it be the proof needed for those who believe life exists elsewhere in the Universe?

Alien found in Israel!

This weird 5-in-long "alien" was discovered in northern Israel in 1998. Clearly visible are a head, legs, arms, and fingers—but could it really be an alien being from another world?

Do aliens exist? If so, they might have heard from us by now—radio and TV signals that were broadcast 50 years ago, and are traveling out from the Earth at 983,571,056 feet per second, have already reached more than 130 stars. Roughly 10% of those stars are likely to have planets—maybe inhabited ones.

Several specially designed radio messages have been sent out into space, in the hope that someone will answer. So why haven't they? Well, perhaps they have—in 1977 a radio signal was received that no one has been able to explain in any other way—it was so surprising that the scientist who received it wrote "Wow!" on the printout.

Wow!

UFO crash

TALK TIME!

In 1967, a ticking radio signal from space was detected. The project to explain it was called "LGM" for "Little Green Men." The source turned out to be a type of spinning star called a pulsar.

Some scientists think that there may be thousands of intelligent civilizations in our galaxy.

In 1960, radio messages were sent to two nearby stars in the hope that intelligent aliens might reply.

More than 30 planets have so far been found in orbit around other stars.

Chatting to aliens on a planet going around another star would need a lot of patience. The nearest such planet goes around a star called Epsilon Eridani, and to send a message there and get a reply back would take 21 years.

is it is it?

EXTRA TERRESTRIALS

Launched in 2009 from Cape Canaveral in Florida, the Kepler telescope is on the lookout for planets in other systems. It will spend at least 3.5 years staring at 100,000 stars in a section of the Milky Way. It's hoped that it will confirm the existence of planets like Earth that are capable of sustaining life.

Claims that this photograph show an alien recovered from a crashed UFO have been put under scrutiny. The crash was said to have taken place in New Mexico in 1950. The picture was sent to Germany for examination and it is believed to be a hoax.

Video recording shown as waves

CODED MESSAGE

The two Voyager spacecraft, both on their way to the stars, are carrying golden discs containing messages for any aliens that might encounter them.

The Voyager and Pioneer space probes should eventually reach other stars, after journeys lasting more than 80,000 years. Plenty of time for them to bump into other beings along the way!

Shows direction of scan needed to play disc

Diagram of hydrogen atom

Location of our Sun

Image of record being played

Index

47

Acknowledgments

COVER (l) © dieter Spears – istockphoto.com, (r) Geoffrey Robinson/Rex Features; **2** Courtesy NASA; **3** (l) © Iuliia Kovalova – fotolia.com, (t/c) Courtesy NASA, (b/c) © Darren Hester – Fotolia.com; **4** (r) NASA, ESA, M. Livio and the Hubble Heritage Team (STScI/AURA); **5** (l) Geoffrey Robinson/Rex Features, (c) © dieter Spears – istockphoto.com, (t/r) Reuters/Richard Carson, (b/l) ESA/Getty Images; **6** (sp) R. Williams (STScI) the Hubble Deep Field Team and NASA; **7** (l) Reuters/Mike Blake, (t/l, t/r, c/l c/r) Rex Features; **8** (t) Courtesy NASA, (b/l) © mario beauregard – fotolia.com, (b/r) Reuters/Ho New; **9** (l) Courtesy of David Hanson, (c) STR/AP/PA Photos, (r) © treenabeena – Fotolia.com; **10–11** (c) © suzannmeer – Fotolia.com; **10** (l) © icholakov – Fotolia.com, (b/l, t/r) Geoeye; **11** (t/l, c, b/r) Geoeye, (t/r) Lewis Whyld/PA Archive/PA Photos; **12** (sp) ESA, (b/r) © suzannmeer – Fotolia.com; **13** (l) Courtesy of Yohkoh Project ISAS/Lockheed–Martin Solar and Astrophysics Laboratory/National Astronomical Observatory of Japan/University of Tokyo/NASA, (b/r) © Ekaterina Starshaya – Fotolia.com; **14** (sp) Courtesy NASA; **15** (c/l) Courtesy NASA, (b/r) Courtesy NASA/JPL–Caltech/Galileo Project, (t/l, t/r, b/l, b/c, b/r) Courtesy NASA; **16** NASA/Johns Hopkins University Applied Physics Laboratory/Carnegie Institution of Washington; **17** (l) Courtesy NASA, (c) Riedrich Saurer/Science Photo Library, (r) Courtesy NASA; **18–19** (sp) Detlev Van Ravenswaay/Science Photo Library; **18** (t/l) NASA; Greg Shirah, SVS, (b/l) Courtesy NASA; **19** (l) NASA/JPL, (r) NASA/JPL–Solar System Visualization Team; **20** (l) A. Simon-Miller/GSFC/NASA/ESA/STScI/Science Photo Library, (r) Copyright Calvin J. Hamilton; **21** (sp) NASA/JPL/Space Science Institute, (r) David Ducros/Science Photo Library; **22** (t) NASA/ESA/L. Sromovsky, U. WISC/STScI/Science Photo Library, (b) Courtesy NASA; **23** (sp) Chris Butler/Science Photo Library, (r) NASA/Kim Shiflett; **24** (l) © Jess Wiberg – istockphoto.com, (r) © Iuliia Kovalova – fotolia.com; **25** (l) © Dennis di Cicco/Corbis, (r) AFP Photo/NASA; **26** (l) © Dragos Constantin – Fotolia.com (c, t) ESA; **27** (l) © Bettmann/Corbis, (r) Courtesy NASA; **28** (sp) NASA, ESA and A. Schaller (for STScI); **29** (t) NASA/JPL–Caltech/T. Megeath (Harvard-Smithsonian CfA), (b) NASA, ESA, A. Feild (STScI); **30** (sp) X-ray: NASA/CXC/CfA/R.Kraft et al.; Submillimeter: MPIfR/ESO/APEX/A.Weiss et al; Optical: ESO/WFI (b/l) NASA/JPL–Caltech/B. Brandl (Cornell & University of Leiden), (b/r) NASA/JPL–Caltech/A. Noriega-Crespo (SSC/Caltech), Digital Sky Survey; **31** (t/l) NASA, NOAO, ESA, Hubble Heritage Team, M. Meixner (STScI) and T.A Rector (NRAO), (t/r) NASA, ESA, HEIC and The Hubble Heritage Team (STScI/AURA), (b, l–r) Courtesy of SOHO/[instrument] consortium. SOHO is a project of international cooperation between ESA and NASA, Matt Bobrowsky (CTA INCORPORATED) and NASA, NASA/JPL–Caltech, The Hubble Heritage Team (STScI/AURA/NASA), H. Bond (STScI), R. Ciardullo (PSU), WFPC2, HST, NASA; **32–33** (sp) Mark Garlick/Science Photo Library; **33** (l) Allan Morton/Dennis Milon/Science Photo Library; **34–35** (dp) NASA/JPL-Caltech/L. Allen (Harvard-Smithsonian CfA), (b) Jean-Charles Cuillandre (CFHT), Hawaiian Starlight, CFHT; **34** (t/l) NASA/JPL–Caltech/P. Morris (NASA Herschel Science Center), (b/l) NASA/JPL–Caltech/J. Rho (SSC/Caltech); **35** (l) NASA/STScI, (r) © Jonathan Larsen – Fotolia.com; **36–37** (dp) Courtesy NASA; **37** (t) Courtesy NASA (c) Rex Features, (b) ESA – S. Corvaja; **38** (sp) © Scott Andrews/Science Faction/Corbis, (l, t, r) Courtesy NASA; **39** (l) Courtesy NASA/Carla Thomas, (r) Courtesy NASA; **40** (l, r) Courtesy NASA; **41** (t/c, t/l, c/l, b/l, b/c/r, r) Courtesy NASA; **42–43** (sp) Courtesy NASA; **42** (b) Courtesy NASA; **43** (t/l) Courtesy NASA, (t/r) Image courtesy of Earth Sciences and Image Analysis Laboratory, NASA Johnson Space Center, ISS Crew, JSC, NASA, (b) Courtesy NASA, (r) © altec5 – fotolia.com; **44** (l) © Snaprender – Fotolia.com, (c/l) Mary Evans Picture Library, (c/r, r) AFP/Getty Images; 45 (l) FPL, (c/l) Courtesy NASA, (c/r) Voyager Project, JPL, NASA, (r) © Darren Hester – Fotolia.com

Key: t = top, b = bottom, c = center, l = left, r = right, sp = single page, dp = double page, bgd = background

Every attempt has been made to acknowledge correctly and contact copyright holders and we apologize in advance for any unintentional errors or omissions, which will be corrected in future editions.